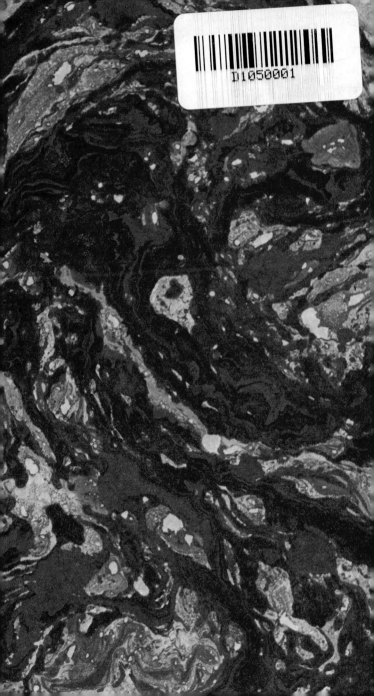

The
Wit and Whimsy
of
Washington Irving

compiled and edited by
Bruce D. MacPhail

The Sleepy Hollow Press
Sleepy Hollow Restorations
Tarrytown, New York

Cover: This professional portrait of Washington Irving, by Charles Martin, engraved by F. Halpin, and dated New York, January, 1851, was said to be one of Irving's favorites.

Title page: Washington Irving sketched this self-portrait at his home, Sunnyside, in Tarrytown, New York, with the Hudson River in the background. The original is signed and dated December 15, 1851.

Text illustrations, except as otherwise noted, by Randolph Caldecott (1846-1886), from the 1876 edition of *Bracebridge Hall,* originally published by Macmillan and Company of London.

PS 2053
M3

Library of Congress Cataloging in Publication Data
Irving, Washington, 1783-1859.
    The wit and whimsy of Washington Irving.
    Bibliography: p.
    I. MacPhail, Bruce D., 1948-   II. Title
PS2053.M3   818'.2'09   79-2567
ISBN 0-912882-37-9

For information, address the publisher:
The Sleepy Hollow Press
Sleepy Hollow Restorations, Inc.
Tarrytown, New York 10591

ISBN 0-912882-37-9
Library of Congress Catalog Card Number 79-2567

Manufactured in the United States of America

Contents

Preface

Washington Irving embraced in his lifetime a wide range of career experiences. As a young man, he worked in his family's trading business, studied law, and was admitted to legal practice. Later, he served as a United States diplomat in England and as U.S. Minister to the Court of Madrid. He was offered a nomination for Mayor of the City of New York, and a cabinet post in the administration of President Martin Van Buren, both of which honors he declined. In his later years, he lived the life of a country gentleman in a charming home which he personally designed and named "Sunnyside."

Today, however, Washington Irving is best remembered as the "Father of American Literature," the first successful American professional man of letters. Writing at first under such now famous pen names as Diedrich Knickerbocker and Geoffrey Crayon, Irving demonstrated a talent for humor and satire. He produced such classic American tales as "Rip Van Winkle" and "The Legend of Sleepy Hollow," and helped to bridge the gap between the established literary traditions of Europe and the emerging culture in the young United States of America.

Throughout his life, Washington Irving sought to comport himself as a gentleman, ever genial and becomingly modest. He enjoyed travel and good company. To his fellow man he was cordial and sympathetic, and he generally regarded the world with a whimsical eye.

Irving's genteel manner and winsome attitude are frequently reflected in his writing. His graceful prose is enlivened by what Irving himself described as a "half concealed vein of humour that is often playing through the whole." Characteristically more pleasant than profound, Irving's most popular works have delighted readers for generations.

This little volume presents a collection of quotations from Washington Irving's published writings and correspondence. As such, it represents a necessarily limited sampling of Irving's rich literary achievements, which many readers will wish to explore more fully, savoring and discovering anew *The Wit and Whimsy of Washington Irving.*

Acknowledgments

The editor would like to acknowledge with appreciation the kind assistance and guidance provided by Professor Ralph M. Aderman of the University of Wisconsin at Milwaukee, Professor Andrew B. Myers of Fordham University, and Professor Richard D. Rust of the University of North Carolina.

Aphorisms for Many Occasions

A TART TEMPER never mellows with age, and a sharp tongue is the only edge tool that grows keener with constant use.

> — *The Sketch Book,*
> "Rip Van Winkle"

As it is universally allowed that a man when drunk sees double, it follows conclusively that he sees twice as well as his sober neighbors.

> — *Knickerbocker's History of New York*, IV, 7

INTO the space of one little hour sins enough may be conjured up by evil tongues to blast the fame of a whole life of virtue.

> — *Wolfert's Roost,*
> "The Widow's Ordeal"

FOR my part, I know no greater delight than to receive letters; but the replying to them is a grievous tax upon my negligent nature. I sometimes think one of the great blessings we shall enjoy in heaven, will be to receive letters by every post and never be obliged to reply to them.

> — letter to Mademoiselle
> Antoinette Bolviller,
> May 28, 1828
> *Life and Letters of*
> *Washington Irving*, II, 319

MANY and many a time have I regretted that at my early outset in life I had not been imperiously bound down to some regular and useful mode of life, and been thoroughly inured to habits of business; and I have a thousand times regretted with bitterness that ever I was led away by my

imagination. Believe me, the man who earns his bread by the sweat of his brow, eats oftener a sweeter morsel, however coarse, than he who procures it by the labor of his brains.

> — letter to
> Reverend Pierre Paris Irving,
> December 7, 1824
> *Life and Letters of
> Washington Irving*, II, 221

GOD BLESS these surgeons and dentists! May their good deeds be returned upon them a thousandfold! May they have the felicity, in the next world, to have successful operations performed upon them to all eternity!

> — letter to a friend (unidentified),
> c. 1844
> *Life and Letters of
> Washington Irving*, III, 341

THERE is nothing like the eye of the master, however active and faithful may be the servants.

> — letter to his sister, Mrs. Paris,
> c. March 1847
> *Life and Letters of
> Washington Irving*, III, 400

EVERY DESIRE bears its death in its very gratification.

— *Bracebridge Hall,*
"The Schoolmaster"

SUSPICION, when once afloat, goes with wind and tide, and soon comes back certainty.

— *Salmagundi,* XVIII

THERE is no one that likes less to be bantered than an absolute joker.

— *Bracebridge Hall,*
"Fortune-Telling"

I HAVE always been something of a castle-builder, and have found my liveliest pleasures to arise from the illusions which fancy has cast over commonplace realities.

— *Bracebridge Hall,*
"Gipsies"

THERE is a certain relief in change even though it be from bad to worse; as I have found in travelling in a stage-coach, that it is often a comfort to shift one's position, and be bruised in a new place.

— *Tales of a Traveller,*
"To the Reader"

On Aging

HAPPY is he who can grow smooth as an old shilling as he wears out; he has endured the rubs of life to some purpose.

— letter to James K. Paulding,
December 24, 1855
Life and Letters of
Washington Irving, IV, 201

I HAVE rarely met with an old gentleman who took absolutely offence at the imputed gallantries of his youth.

— *The Sketch Book,*
"The Christmas Dinner"

TIME is not such an invariable destroyer as he is represented. . . . Under his plastic hand trifles rise into importance; the nonsense of one age becomes the wisdom of another; the levity of the wit gravitates into the learning of the pedant, and an ancient farthing moulders into infinitely more value than a modern guinea.

— *Bracebridge Hall,*
"A Literary Antiquary"

WHENEVER a man's friends begin to compliment him about looking young, he may be sure that they think he is growing old.
— *Bracebridge Hall,*
"Bachelors"

THERE is no character in the comedy of human life that is more difficult to play well than that of an old bachelor.
— *Bracebridge Hall,*
"Bachelors"

THE general, in fact, has arrived at that time of life when the heart and the stomach maintain a kind of balance of power; and when a man is apt to be perplexed in his affections between a fine woman and a truffled turkey.

— *Bracebridge Hall,*
"The Wedding"

On Good Fortune
and Misfortune

IF we could but get a peep at the tally of dame Fortune, where like a vigilant landlady she chalks up the debtor and creditor accounts of thoughtless mortals, we should find that every good is checked off by an evil; and that however we may apparently revel scotfree for a season, the time will come when we must ruefully pay off the reckoning.

— *Knickerbocker's History of New York*, IV, 9

WE are none of us completely sheltered from misfortune. If we do not put to sea, the sea overflows its bounds and drowns us on the land. For my own part, with all my exertions, I seem always to keep about up to my chin in troubled water, while the world, I suppose, thinks I am sailing smoothly with the wind and tide in my favour.

— *Letters to Brevoort,*
February 23, 1828

LITTLE MINDS are tamed and subdued by misfortune; but great minds rise above it.

— *The Sketch Book,*
"Philip of Pokanoket"

THERE is nothing so convenient as this "some how or other" way of accommodating one's self to circumstances; it is the main stay of a heedless actor, and tardy reasoner . . . and he who can, in this loose, easy way, link foregone evil to anticipated good, possesses a secret of happiness almost equal to the philosopher's stone.

— *Bracebridge Hall,*
"Dolph Heyliger"

On History

THE MOST GLORIOUS hero that ever deso-
lated nations might have mouldered into
oblivion among the rubbish of his own
monument, did not some historian take
him into favor, and benevolently transmit
his name to posterity.

> — *Knickerbocker's History
> of New York*, V, 1

FOR what is history, in fact, but a kind of
Newgate calendar, a register of the crimes
and miseries that man has inflicted on his
fellow man? It is a huge libel on human
nature, to which we industriously add
page after page, volume after volume, as
if we were building up a monument to the
honor, rather than the infamy of the
species.

> — *Knickerbocker's History
> of New York*, IV, 1

On Human Nature

FOR my part, I have not so bad an opinion
of mankind as many of my brother phil-
osophers. I do not think poor human nature so sorry a piece of workmanship as
they would make it out to be; and as far
as I have observed, I am fully satisfied
that man, if left to himself, would about
as readily go right as wrong. It is only this
eternally sounding in his ears that it is
his duty to go right, which makes him go
the very reverse.

> — *Knickerbocker's History
> of New York*, II, 8

THERE are few happier beings than a
busy idler; that is to say, a man who is
eternally busy about nothing.

> — *Bracebridge Hall,*
> "The Busy Man"

THOSE MEN are most apt to be obsequious and conciliating abroad, who are under the discipline of shrews at home.

> — *The Sketch Book,*
> "Rip Van Winkle"

WHO EVER hears of fat men heading a riot, or herding together in turbulent mobs? —no —no, it is your lean, hungry men who are continually worrying society, and setting the whole community by the ears.

> — *Knickerbocker's History
> of New York,* III, 2

IN ALL situations of life into which I have looked, I have found mankind divided into two grand parties: those who ride, and those who are ridden. The great struggle of life seems to be which shall keep in the saddle.

> — *Tales of a Traveller,*
> "Buckthorne"

HE who never leaves home repines at his monotonous existence, and envies the traveler, whose life is a constant tissue of wonder and adventure; while he who is tossed about the world, looks back with

many a sigh to the safe and quiet shore
which he has abandoned.
> — *Bracebridge Hall,*
> "The Schoolmaster"

WE are always regretting the past, or lan-
guishing for the distant; every spot is
fresh and green but the one we stand on.
> — *Letters to Brevoort,*
> March 15, 1816

HE who has sought renown about the
world, and has reaped a full harvest of
worldly favor, will find, after all, that
there is no love, no admiration, no ap-
plause, so sweet to the soul as that which
springs up in his native place.
> — *The Sketch Book,*
> "Stratford-on-Avon"

THE SORROW for the dead is the only sorrow from which we refuse to be divorced.
Every other wound we seek to heal—every
other affliction to forget; but this wound
we consider it a duty to keep open—this
affliction we cherish and brood over in
solitude.
> — *The Sketch Book,*
> "Rural Funerals"

MEN are apt to acquire peculiarities that are continually ascribed to them.

> — *The Sketch Book,*
> "John Bull"

THE WORLD has become more worldly. There is more of dissipation, and less of enjoyment. Pleasure has expanded into a broader, but a shallower stream, and has forsaken many of those deep and quiet channels where it flowed sweetly through the calm bosom of domestic life.

> — *The Sketch Book,*
> "Christmas"

IN CIVILIZED LIFE, where the happiness, and indeed almost the existence, of man depends so much upon the opinion of his fellow-men, he is constantly acting a studied part.

> — *The Sketch Book,*
> "Philip of Pokanoket"

No MAN is so methodical as a complete idler, and none so scrupulous in measuring out his time as he whose time is worth nothing.

> — *Wolfert's Roost,*
> "My French Neighbor"

THERE is nothing so difficult to conquer as the vagrant humour, when once it has been fully indulged.
> — *Bracebridge Hall*,
> "The Schoolmaster"

IT SEEMS to me worth the pain of sending children from home for a while, to have the joy of getting them back again.
> — letter to Sarah Storrow,
> December 1, 1827
> *Washington Irving and
> the Storrows*

On Humility

MUCH as we may think of ourselves, and much as we may excite the empty plaudits of the million, it is certain that the greatest among us do actually fill but an exceeding small space in the world; and it is equally certain, that even that small space is quickly supplied when we leave it vacant.

— *Knickerbocker's History of New York*, V, 1

HE who is on the uppermost round of a ladder has most to suffer from a fall, while he who is at the bottom runs very little risk of breaking his neck by tumbling to the top.

— *Knickerbocker's History of New York*, IV, 9

I HAVE the same feeling in this respect that I have always had on points of precedence; I care not who takes the lead of me in entering an apartment, or sits above me at table. It is better that half a dozen should say why is he seated so low down, than any one should casually say what right has he to be at the top.

> — letter to Peter Irving,
> July 25, 1829
> *Life and Letters
> of Washington Irving*, II, 405

THOSE who are well assured of their own standing are least apt to trespass on that of others; whereas nothing is so offensive as the aspirings of vulgarity, which thinks to elevate itself by humiliating its neighbor.

> — *The Sketch Book,*
> "The Country Church"

On Learning and Wisdom

I FEEL convinced that the true interests and solid happiness of man are promoted by the advancement of truth; yet I cannot but mourn over the pleasant errors which it has trampled down in its progress.

— *Bracebridge Hall,*
"Popular Superstitions"

A MAN . . . who talks good sense in his native tongue, is held in tolerable estimation in this country; but a fool, who clothes his feeble ideas in a foreign or antique garb, is bowed down to, as a literary prodigy.

— *Salmagundi,* VII

THEORIES are the mighty soap bubbles with which the grown up children of science amuse themselves—while the honest vulgar stand gazing in stupid admiration, and dignify these learned vagaries with the name of wisdom.

— *Knickerbocker's History of New York,* I, 2

IT IS IN KNOWLEDGE as in swimming; he who flounders and splashes on the surface, makes more noise, and attracts more attention, than the pearl-diver who quietly dives in quest of treasures to the bottom.

*— Knickerbocker's History
of New York*, IV, 1

A LITTLE SOUND JUDGMENT and plain common sense is worth all the sparkling genius that ever wrote poetry or invented theories.

*— Knickerbocker's History
of New York*, IV, 1

On Literature

AN early, innocent, and unfortunate passion, however fruitful of pain it may be to the man, is a lasting advantage to the poet. It is a well of sweet and bitter fancies; of refined and gentle sentiments; of elevated and ennobling thoughts; shut up in the deep recesses of the heart, keeping it green amidst the withering blights of the world, and, by its casual gushings and overflowings, recalling at times all the freshness, and innocence, and enthusiasm of youthful days.

— *The Crayon Miscellany,*
"Newstead Abbey"
(Annesley Hall)

MY cousin . . . declared that it was as necessary for a modern poet to have an assistant, as for Don Quixote to have a Sancho—that it was the fashion for poets, now-a-days, to write so ineffably obscure, that every line required a page of notes to explain its meaning.

— *Salmagundi*, IV

Our literature, before long, will be like some of those premature and aspiring whipsters, who become old men before they are young ones, and fancy they prove their manhood by their profligacy and their diseases.

— *Letters to Brevoort,*
December 20, 1828

"The Author in Westminster Abbey," by Edwin White, from the 1868 "Artist's Edition" of Irving's *Sketch Book*, published by G.P. Putnam, New York.

LANGUAGE gradually varies, and with it fade away the writings of authors who have flourished their allotted time; otherwise, the creative powers of genius would overstock the world, and the mind would be completely bewildered in the endless mazes of literature.

— *The Sketch Book*,
   "The Mutability of Literature"

THERE RISE AUTHORS now and then, who seem proof against the mutability of language, because they have rooted themselves in the unchanging principles of human nature.

— *The Sketch Book*,
   "The Mutability of Literature"

DO NOT read for the purpose of mere conversation the popular works of the day, reviews, magazines, etc. Be content to appear ignorant of those topics rather than read through fear of appearing ignorant. The literature of the day is always the most *piquant*, the most immediately interesting, but is generally transient; it soon passes away and leaves no general knowledge, no permanent topic in the mind;

and then it is so *copious*; if one yield his attention to contemporary literature, he is overwhelmed with it. Make yourself, on the other hand, well acquainted with the valuable standard authors, which have stood the test of time; they will always be in fashion; and in becoming intimately acquainted with them, you become intimately acquainted with the principles of knowledge and good taste.

— letter to Pierre Paris Irving,
March 29, 1825
*Life and Letters
of Washington Irving*, II, 235

THE LITERARY WORLD is made up of little confederacies, each looking upon its own members as the lights of the universe; and considering all others as mere transient meteors, doomed soon to fall and be forgotten, while its own luminaries are to shine steadily on to immortality.

— *Tales of a Traveller*,
"Literary Life"

On Nature

THERE ARE HOMILIES in nature's works
worth all the wisdom of the schools, if we
could but read them rightly, and one of
the pleasantest lessons I ever received in
time of trouble, was from hearing the
notes of a lark.

> — *Tales of a Traveller,*
> "A Practical Philosopher"

SUCH is the glorious independence of man
in a savage state. This youth, with his rifle,
his blanket, and his horse, was ready at a
moment's warning to rove the world; he
carried all his worldly effects with him,
and in the absence of artificial wants,
possessed the great secret of personal free-
dom. We of society are slaves, not so much
to others as to ourselves; our superfluities
are the chains that bind us, impeding

"Trout Stream," engraved by J.H. Richardson after an original by William Hart, from the "Artist's Edition" of Irving's *Sketch Book*.

every movement of our bodies and thwarting every impulse of our souls.
— *The Crayon Miscellany*,
"A Tour on the Prairies"

FOR my part, . . . I keep outdoors, and busy myself about the garden and the fields all day, whenever not absolutely driven in by the rain—so that when evening comes I am completely fagged, and am apt to doze over my book in the drawing room; but then I gain a good night's sleep, and that is always worth working for.

— letter to Sarah Storrow,
May 8, 1841
*Letters from
Sunnyside and Spain*

THERE is certainly something in angling ... that tends to produce a gentleness of spirit, and a pure serenity of mind.

— *The Sketch Book,*
"The Angler"

IT WAS that delicious season of the year, when nature, breaking from the chilling thraldom of old winter, like a blooming damsel from the tyranny of a sordid old father, threw herself, blushing with ten thousand charms, into the arms of youthful spring.

— *Knickerbocker's History
of New York,* II, 4

THE BLESSED breath of Spring ... is sufficient to thaw the inmost fountains of the heart and set all the affections in a flow.

— letter to Sarah Storrow,
May 8, 1841
*Letters from
Sunnyside and Spain*

Diedrich Knickerbocker, one of Irving's most amiable and optimistic characters, by William Strickland, from the second edition of *A History of New York* (1812).

On Optimism
and Amiability

I HAVE always had an opinion that much good might be done by keeping mankind in good humor with one another. . . . When I discover the world to be all that it has been represented by sneering cynics and whining poets, I will turn to and abuse it also; in the meanwhile, worthy reader, I hope you will not think lightly of me, because I cannot believe this to be so very bad a world as it is represented.

— *Bracebridge Hall,*
"The Author"

I HAVE too high an opinion of the understanding of my fellow-citizens, to think of yielding them instruction, and I covet too much their good will, to forfeit it by giving them good advice. I am none of those cynics who despise the world, because it despises them—on the contrary, though but low in its regard, I look up to it with the most perfect good nature, and my only sorrow is, that it does not prove itself more worthy of the unbounded love I bear it.

— *Knickerbocker's History of New York*, VII, 13

A cheerful tavern scene, by Arthur Rackham, from an illustrated edition of *Rip Van Winkle* (New York and London, 1905).

FOR my part, I endeavor to take things as they come with cheerfulness, and when I cannot get a dinner to suit my taste, I endeavor to get a taste to suit my dinner.

> — letter to William Irving,
>   c. September 10, 1804
>   *Life and Letters
>   of Washington Irving*, I, 78-79

I AM for curing the world by gentle alternatives, not by violent doses; indeed, the patient should never be conscious that he is taking a dose.

> — *Tales of a Traveller*,
>   "To the Reader"

WE FANCY others feel the sunshine that is only in our bosoms, and, while full of good humor and good will, the idea never enters one's mind that even one's good humor may be irksome.

> — letter to Mrs. Amelia Foster,
>   May 23, 1823
>   *Life and Letters
>   of Washington Irving*, IV, 391

HAPPINESS is reflective, like the light of heaven; and every countenance, bright with smiles, and glowing with innocent enjoyment, is a mirror transmitting to others the rays of a supreme and ever-shining benevolence.

— *The Sketch Book,*
"Christmas"

WIT, after all, is a mighty, tart, pungent ingredient, and much too acid for some stomachs; but honest good humor is the oil and wine of a merry meeting, and there is no jovial companionship equal to that where the jokes are rather small and the laughter abundant.

— *The Sketch Book,*
"The Christmas Dinner"

I LIKE a man of sense, who, now and then, in the fullness of his heart, does things to make one smile. He is worth a dozen of those coolheaded, wary fellows, that never do a foolish thing; they as seldom do a kind one.

— letter to Mrs. Amelia Foster,
June 13, 1823
*Life and Letters
of Washington Irving,* IV, 403

On Politics
and Public Office

THE GREAT OBJECT of our political disputes is, not who shall have the *honour* of emancipating the community from the leading-strings of delusion, but who shall have the *profit* of holding the strings, and leading the community by the nose.
— *Salmagundi*, XV

YOUR TRUE DULL MINDS are generally preferred for public employ, and especially promoted to city honors; your keen intellects, like razors, being considered too sharp for common service.
— *Knickerbocker's History
of New York*, III, 2

IT IS THE MYSTERY which envelops great men, that gives them half their greatness. There is a kind of superstitious reverence for office which leads us to exaggerate the merits of the occupant; and to suppose that he must be wiser than common men.

— *Knickerbocker's History of New York*, VII, 1

On Pride and Vanity

How CONVENIENT it would be to many of our great men and great families of doubtful origin, could they have the privilege of the heroes of yore, who, whenever their origin was involved in obscurity, modestly announced themselves descended from a god.

> — *Knickerbocker's History of New York*, II, 3

WHAT A PITY they could not content themselves with seeing all that was instructive, interesting and delightful in Europe, and returning home cultivated in taste, enriched in thought and stored with agreeable recollections for the rest of their lives—How erroneous for Americans to come to Paris not to *see* but to be *seen*.

> — letter to Sarah Storrow,
> January 5, 1843
> *Letters to Sarah Storrow*

"The Sermon," by Randolph Caldecott, from the 1875 edition of *Old Christmas*, published by Macmillan and Company of London.

On Religion

A CUNNING POLITICIAN often lurks under the clerical robe; things spiritual and things temporal are strangely jumbled together, like drugs on an apothecary's shelf; and instead of a peaceful sermon, the simple seeker after righteousness has often a political pamphlet thrust down his throat, labeled with a pious text from Scripture.

> — *Knickerbocker's History of New York*, V, 7

(Writing of the Old Dutch Church of Sleepy Hollow:)

Two weathercocks, with the initials of these illustrious personages, graced each end of the church, one perched over the belfry, the other over the chancel. As usual with ecclesiastical weathercocks, each pointed a different way; and there was a perpetual contradiction between them on all points of windy doctrine; emblematic, alas! of the Christian propensity to schism and controversy.

— *Wolfert's Roost,*
"Wolfert's Roost"

The Old Dutch Church of Sleepy Hollow, by Edgar Mayhew Bacon (1855-1935).

On Wealth and Economy

To ME a dry crust paid for is a sweeter morsel than a truffled turkey that I have run in debt for.

> — letter to John Howard Payne,
> December 25, 1825
> Collections of the
> Columbia University Library

As TO his circumstances, he has only to practice a little rigid economy—to stand still as it were, for a while and let his means overtake him.

> — letter to C. B. Coles,
> December 31, 1825
> Collection of Andrew B. Myers

A FEW ribbands fancifully disposed can constitute a passable fancy dress.

> — letter to his six nieces,
> February 4, 1840
> *Letters from*
> *Sunnyside and Spain*

FOR A LONG TIME he was suspected of being crazy, and then every body pitied him; at length it began to be suspected that he was poor, and then every body avoided him.

— *Tales of a Traveller,*
"Wolfert Webber"

THANK HEAVEN! I was brought up in simple and inexpensive habits, and I have satisfied myself that, if need be, I can resume them without repining or inconvenience. Though I am willing, therefore, that fortune should shower her blessings upon me, and think I can enjoy them as well as most men, I shall not make myself unhappy if she chooses to be scanty, and shall take the position allotted me with a cheerful and contented mind.

— letter to Henry Brevoort,
December 9, 1816
*Life and Letters
of Washington Irving*

IN A WORD, the almighty dollar, that great object of universal devotion throughout our land, seems to have no genuine devotees in these peculiar villages; and unless some of its missionaries penetrate there, and erect banking houses and other pious shrines, there is no knowing how long the inhabitants may remain in their present state of contented poverty.

— *Wolfert's Roost,*
"The Creole Village"

SPECULATION is the romance of trade, and casts contempt upon all its sober realities. It renders the stock-jobber a magician, and the exchange a region of enchantment. It elevates the merchant into a king or knight-errant, or rather a commercial Quixote.

— *Wolfert's Roost,*
"A Time of Unexampled Prosperity"

IT IS NOT POVERTY so much as pretence, that harasses a ruined man. . . . Have the courage to appear poor and you disarm poverty of its sharpest sting.

> — *The Sketch Book,*
> "The Wife"

HE LIVES like a man of sense, who knows he can but enjoy his money when he is alive, and would not be a whit the better though he were buried under a mountain of it when dead.

> — letter to Ebenezer Irving,
> August, 1815
> *Life and Letters
> of Washington Irving*, I, 333

On Women and Marriage

No WOMAN can expect to be to her husband all that he fancied her when he was a lover. Men are always doomed to be duped, not so much by the arts of the sex, as by their own imaginations. They are always wooing goddesses, and marrying mere mortals.

> — *Bracebridge Hall,*
> "Wives"

A PRETTY country retreat is like a pretty wife—one is always throwing away money in decorating it.

> — letter to Mrs. John P. Kennedy,
> c. November, 1853
> *Life and Letters*
> *of Washington Irving,* IV, 167

His wife "ruled the roast," and in governing the governor, governed the province, which might thus be said to be under petticoat government.

— *Knickerbocker's History of New York*, IV, 4

No one can accuse her of devotion to her own husband, though she is said to be full of loving kindness to all mankind beside.

— letter to Sarah Storrow, February 10, 1844
Letters to Sarah Storrow

You ARE like a bark without an anchor, that drifts about at the mercy of every vagrant breeze, or trifling eddy — get a wife and she'll anchor you.

> — *Letters to Brevoort,*
> March 15, 1816

A MARRIED MAN, with his wife hanging on his arm, always puts [me] in mind of a chamber candlestick, with its extinguisher hitched to it.

> — *Bracebridge Hall,*
> "Bachelors"

THE GENTLE SEX in all ages have shown the same disposition to infringe a little upon the laws of decorum, in order to betray a lurking beauty, or gratify an innocent love of finery.

> — *Knickerbocker's History of New York*, III, 4

THERE IS in every true woman's heart a spark of heavenly fire, which lies dormant in the broad daylight of prosperity; but which kindles up, and beams and blazes in the dark hour of adversity.

> — *The Sketch Book,*
> "The Wife"

OUR GOOD GRANDMOTHERS differed considerably in their ideas of a fine figure from their scantily dressed descendants of the present day. A fine lady, in those times, waddled under more clothes, even on a summer's day, than would have clad the whole bevy of a modern ball-room.

— *Knickerbocker's History of New York*, III, 4

THERE certainly is a selfish pleasure in possessing a thing which is exclusively our own and which we see everybody around us coveting. And this may be the reason why we sometimes behold very beautiful women maintaining resolute possession of their charms—and what makes me think this must be the reason is that in proportion as these women grow old, and the world ceases to long after their treasures, they seem the most ready to part with them, until they at length seem ready to sacrifice them to the first bidder, and even to importune you to take them off their hands.

— *Letters to Brevoort*, July 8, 1812

A WOMAN'S WHOLE LIFE is a history of the affections.

— *The Sketch Book,*
"The Broken Heart"

THE SENTIMENT OF LOVE may be, and is, in a great measure, a fostered growth of poetry and romance, and balderdashed with false sentiment; but, with all its vitiations, it is the beauty and charm, the flavor and fragrance of all intercourse between man and woman; it is the rosy cloud in the morning of life; and if it does too often resolve itself into the shower, yet to my mind, it only makes our nature more fruitful in what is excellent and amiable.

— letter to Mrs. Amelia Foster,
May 28, 1823
*Life and Letters
of Washington Irving,*
IV, 390-91

"Irving's Study," by Benson J. Lossing (1818-1890).

On Writing
and Publishing

THE LAND of literature is a fairy land to those who view it at a distance, but, like all other landscapes, the charm fades on a nearer approach, and the thorns and briers become visible. The republic of letters is the most factious and discordant of all republics, ancient or modern.

> — *Tales of a Traveller,*
> "Notoriety"

THE ONLY HAPPY AUTHOR in this world is he who is below the care of reputation.

> — *Tales of a Traveller,*
> "The Poor-Devil Author"

I SHOULD LIKE to write occasionally for my amusement, and to have the power of throwing my writings either into my portfolio, or into the fire. I enjoy the first conception and first sketchings down of my ideas, but the correcting and preparing of them for the press is irksome, and publishing is detestable.

> — letter to Henry Brevoort,
> December 11, 1824
> *Life and Letters*
> *of Washington Irving*, II, 226

COULD I afford it, I should like to write and lay my writings aside when finished. There is an independent delight in study and in the creative exercise of the pen; we live in a world of dreams, but publication lets in the noisy rabble of the world and there is an end to our dreaming.

> — *Letters to Brevoort*,
> April 4, 1827

A Final Thought

IF, however, I can by any lucky chance, in these days of evil, rub out one wrinkle from the brow of care, or beguile the heavy heart of one moment of sorrow; if I can now and then penetrate through the gathering film of misanthropy, prompt a benevolent view of human nature, and make my reader more in good humor with his fellow beings and himself, surely, surely, I shall not then have written entirely in vain.

— *The Sketch Book,*
   "The Christmas Dinner"

Bibliography

Irving, Pierre M. *The Life and Letters of Washington Irving.* 4 vols. New York: G. P. Putnam, 1862-1864.

Irving, Washington. *Letters from Sunnyside and Spain.* Edited by Stanley T. Williams. New Haven: Yale University Press, 1928.

————. *Letters of Washington Irving to Henry Brevoort.* Edited by George S. Hellman. New York: G. P. Putnam, 1915. 2 vols.

————. "Letters to Sarah Storrow from Spain." Edited by Barbara D. Simison. Papers in Honor of Andrew Keogh, edited by the Staff of the Yale University Library. New Haven: privately printed, 1938.

————. *Washington Irving and the Storrows: Letters from England and the Continent, 1821-1828.* Edited by Stanley T. Williams. Cambridge, Mass.: Harvard University Press, 1933.

————. *The Works of Washington Irving.* Author's Revised Edition. New York: G. P. Putnam, 1848-1850.

Irving, Washington, with William Irving and James Kirk Paulding. *Salmagundi: Or, The Whim-Whams and Opinions of Launcelot Langstaff, Esq., and Others.* Edited by Evert A. Duyckinck. New York: G. P. Putnam, 1860.

Sleepy Hollow Restorations, Inc., is a non-profit educational institution chartered by the Board of Regents of the University of the State of New York. Established under an endowment provided, in large part, by the late John D. Rockefeller, Jr., Sleepy Hollow Restorations owns and maintains *Sunnyside*, Washington Irving's picturesque home in Tarrytown; *Philipsburg Manor, Upper Mills*, a colonial commercial mill complex in North Tarrytown; and *Van Cortlandt Manor*, a distinguished eighteenth-century family estate in Croton-on-Hudson.

The Wit and Whimsy of Washington Irving is set in an old style type face of the Bodoni family, especially popular in the nineteenth century. The type was composed by Crescent Typographers of New York City.

The original illustrations beginning each section and illuminating the folio numbers, and the design for the cover and endpapers, are by Edward J. McLaughlin of Washingtonville, New York.

Other text illustrations were reproduced with all possible precision from originals which appeared in special editions of the works of Washington Irving.

This book was printed by Aristographics, Inc., of New York City, and bound by The Haddon Craftsmen of Scranton, Pennsylvania.